Chapter

YAH'S Seven Witnesses

YAH's Seven Witness

According to the Holy Scriptures any matter that arises in YisraEL had to be established by the mouth of two or three witnesses. Read Deuteronomy 19v15, Deuteronomy 17v7, Genesis 41v32. Also II Chronicles 20v20 reads: So they rose early in the morning and went out into the wilderness of Tekoa; and as they went out, Jehoshaphat stood and said, Hear me O Judah and you inhabitants of Jerusalem: believe in YAHWEH your ELOHIM and you shall be established; believe his prophets' and you shall prosper.

These are the Seven Witnesses that establish and prove that there is 30 days in EVERY month and 12 months in EVERY year According to the scriptures. Also the Hebrew word for twelve is Shenayim (8147) - Dual of (8145) - to do again, twice, to duplicate, to fold. This is derived from the Hebrew word Shanah (8138) which is the same word for Year.

1. *Noah*-Noah was considered one of the three most righteous men that ever lived. (Ezekiel 14v14-19). During the time of the flood when the fountains of the great deep were broken up, and the windows of heaven were opened Noah and his family entered the Ark the **Second Month on the Seventeenth day of the Month. (**Genesis 7v11-13) Then YAH remembered Noah and every living thing on the Ark, after the fountains of the deep and windows of the heaven were stopped, and the rain from heaven were restrained. The waters receded continually from the earth at the end of **150 days** so the ark rested in the **Seventh Month the Seventeenth day of the Month** on the Mountains of Ararat. **(2nd Month 17th day of the Month through the 7th Month the 17th Day of the Month is 150 days. 30 days a month over the span of 5 months.)**
2. *Moses*- Moses was considered the greatest prophet that ever lived and the meekest man in the Most High House. (Numbers 12v3 and also Deuteronomy 34v10-12). According to the Scriptures we only had one manner of law for the home born and the stranger. (Numbers 15v29-30). When our people went to war with our enemies and we see among the captives a beautiful woman that we desired to take her for a wife we were to shave her head, pair her nails, and allow her to **mourn** her parents a **full month**. Since we only had one Law for the stranger and the home born, a **full month** is explained with Moses in his **mourning** period after his death, which was **30 days.** (Deuteronomy 34v8)
3. *Aaron*- Aaron was the High Priest of the Most High, YAH established his Priest hood forever (Jeremiah 33v17-22 Exodus 29v9) Aaron Mourning Period was also 30 days. (Number 20v29)
4. *David*- David was YAH beloved King whom YAH said David was a man after his own heart. His kingdom was prophesied to return on earth and David would be the King of Kings, Higher than all the kings of the earth. Read (I Samuel 13v14, Ezekiel 37v21-28, Psalm 89v19-29). The children of YisraEL according to their number, the heads of father's houses served the king in EVERY

matter, and they came in and went out Month to Month throughout ALL the Months of the year. (I Chronicles 27v1-15) **12 Divisions for 12 months**

5. ***Solomon*-** King Solomon was said to be wiser than all men, his wisdom and understanding was exceedingly great. His wisdom excelled the wisdom of all men of the east and all the wisdom of Egypt (I King 4v29-34). King Solomon had 12 governors over all YisraEL who provided food for the king household each one made provision for one Month of the year. Read(I king 4v7) **12 Governors for 12 Months**

6. ***Daniel*-** Daniel was considered one of the three most Righteous men that ever lived. He was skilled in all manner of wisdom, possessing knowledge and quick to understand. (Ezekiel 14v14-19, Daniel 1v4) Daniel spoke of a vision that he had on his bed and the vision let King Nebuchadnezzar know that if he did not acknowledge the Most High that his kingdom would depart and he would live as a wild beast eating grass. Daniel Revealed that after 12 months ended that the king began to **eat grass** like oxen for seven years.(Daniel 4v27-34)

7. The last witness concerning how many days are in a month and how many months are in a year is greater than all the other witnesses put together. The **Seventh witness is YAHWEH himself**, for **YAH** stated that his people will be in the Wilderness for 40 years, also those 40 years they would eat manna as a sign and test to see if they would keep his law or not. (Deuteronomy 8v1-5) The children of YisraEL left Egypt the morrow after the Passover at night, **(which was the 15th of the 1st Month,** Deuteronomy 16v1, Numbers 33v3). The **children of YisraEL began to dwell in the wilderness on the 1st Month 16th day of the Month; they also began to eat manna on the 2nd Month 16th day of the Month. (Exodus 14v1-30, Exodus 16v1-35)** After Joshua circumcised the males coming out of Egypt 40 years later, YAHWEH rolled away the reproach of Egypt and they kept the Passover on the 14th, ate the produce of the land on the 15th **and the manna ceased on the 16th 40 years later.** They also encamped out of the wilderness this same day at the wall of Jericho. (Joshua 5v10-15). **The 1st year 16th day through the 16th, 40 years later = a precise 30 days a month and 12 months a year.**

NOTE: Although many teachers teach that there are some months that are 29 days in duration and 13 months in some years there are no scriptures founded to support these claims.

Chapter 2

The New Moon
or
The New Month

FOREWORD

According to the Holy Scriptures in the book of **Genesis 1v14** *"And Elohim said, let there be lights in the firmament of the heaven to divide the day from the night: and let them be for signs, and for seasons, and for days, and years; and let them be for lights in the firmament of the heaven to give light upon the earth; And it was so And Elohim made two great lights: the greater light to rule the day and the lesser light to rule the night: he made the stars also. And Elohim set them in the firmament of the heaven to give light upon the earth, And to rule over the day and over the night, and to divide the light from the darkness and Elohim saw that it was good."*

In the world of religions it is commonly taught that a day begins in the evening or the night. Since this is the popular held belief it is also believed that the moon, which is a light by night, is made for the months and the years. I will prove beyond a shadow of a doubt that when YAHWEH made the lights they were not for the reasons taught by the other nations or their religions. One of the chief religions that has contributed to the confusion of how the lights are interpreted in the scriptures, is called Judaism. In Judaism, not only the day begins in the evening, right before the night but the months also begins in the evening during the time of the crescent moon, which is believed to mark the beginning of the month. According to the Holy Scriptures we will prove beyond a shadow of a doubt what the moon is made for and it's appointed time.

THE ABIB

According to the Holy Scriptures the word Abib is mentioned approximately seven times. In some Jewish and Christian sects they look for the Abib to determine when the Biblical New Year begins. The word Abib means green ears or ears of grains. When the word Abib is mentioned it is never mentioned in connection with the beginning of the month but it is always mentioned at the time of Passover as well as the Feast of Unleavened Bread, which is the 14th and 15th of the month.

Some examples of how the word Abib is used in the scriptures, are as follows;

Exodus 13v3-4 "And Moses said unto the people, remember this day in which ye came out from Egypt, out of the house of bondage: for by strength of hand YAH brought you out from this place: there shall no leavened bread be eaten. This day came ye out in the month Abib."

Exodus 23v14-15 "Three times thou shalt keep a feast unto me in the year. Thou shalt keep the Feast of Unleavened Bread: thou shalt eat unleavened bread seven days, as I commanded thee, in the time appointed of the month of Abib; for in it thou camest out from Egypt: and none shall appear before me empty."

Exodus 34v18 "The Feast of Unleavened Bread shalt thou keep. Seven days thou shalt eat unleavened bread, as I commanded thee in the time of the month Abib: in the month Abib thou camest out from Egypt."

Deuteronomy 16v1 "Observe the month of Abib and keep the Passover unto YAH thy Elohim: for in the month of Abib YAH thy Elohim brought thee forth out of Egypt by night."

It is clear from the scriptures that the month of Abib was to be observed for bringing the children of YisraEL out of Egypt by night and this was the night to be much observed. Also, read **Exodus 12v40-42** "Now the sojourning fo the children of YisraEL who dwelt in Egypt, was four hundred and thirty years. And it came to pass at the end of the four hundred and thirty years, even the selfsame day it came to pass that all the host of YAH went out from the land of Egypt. It is a night to be much observed unto YAH for bringing them out from the land of Egypt, this is that night of YAH to be observed of all the children of YisraEL in their generations."

The night that YAHWEH wanted observed was not the beginning of the month of Abib as commonly taught and believed but rather the 15th day of the month at night.

THE MOON FOR SEASONS

Psalm 104v19-20 *"He appointed the moon for seasons: the sun knoweth his going down. Thou makest darkness and it is night: wherein all the beast of the forest do creep forth."*

According to the scriptures when YAHWEH made the lights for signs, seasons, days, and years. He made the Sun to rule the day and the Moon and the Stars to rule the night. The lesser light that YAHWEH made for the night is called the Moon. The Hebrew word for Moon is Yareach. I will prove beyond a shadow of a doubt, through the scriptures of the truth, that the Moon was not for the days of the month. Neither was the Moon made for days, period. All through the Scriptures YAHWEH states the Moon is a light by night, a light to separate the day from the night, and a light for the night season.

Please read Ps 22: 1-2 My Elohim, my Elohim, why hast thou forsaken me ? *Why art thou so far from helping me, and from* the words of my roaring ? 2 O my Elohim, I cry in the daytime, but thou hearest not; and in the night season, and am not silent.

Genesis 1v16 *"And Elohim made two great lights; the greater light to rule the Day and the lesser light to rule the Night; he made the stars also."*

Psalm 136v7-9 *"To him that made great lights: for his mercy endureth for ever: The sun to rule by day: for his mercy endureth for ever: The moon and stars to rule by night: for his mercy endureth for ever:"*

Psalm 121v6 *"The sun shall not smite thee by day, nor the moon by night."*

YAHWEH also made a covenant with the Moon:

Jeremiah 31v35-36 *"Thus saith YAH, which giveth Sun for a light by day, and the ordinances of the Moon and of the stars for a light by night; which divideth the sea when the waves there of roar: YAH of host is his name: If these ordinances depart from before me, saith YAH then the seed of YisraEL also shall cease from being a nation before me for ever."*

Jeremiah 33v20-21 *"Thus saith YAH, if ye can break my covenant of the day, and my covenant of the night, and that there should not be day and night in their season: Then may also my covenant be broken with David my servant, that he should not have a son to reign upon his throne; and with the Levites the priests, my ministers."*

It is clear from these Scriptures that the season of the Moon is set for the night rather than a sign for the day.

30 DAYS A MONTH

According to the Holy Scriptures a month is a set number of days. It is commonly taught that a month in the scriptures mean Moon and that a Moon means month. However, the Hebrew word for month is Chodesh and the Hebrew word for Moon is Yareach. The Hebrew word Yareach is never referred to as a month or Chodesh in the scriptures, it is always translated as moon. The Hebrew word Chodesh is sometimes translated as New Moon, which is erroneous and deceptive.

Deuteronomy 21v10-14 *"When thou goest forth to war against thine enemies, and YAHWEH thy Elohim hath delivered them into thine hands, and thou hast taken them captive. And seest among the captives a beautiful woman, and hast a desire unto her, that thou wouldest have her to thy wife; then thou shalt bring her home to thine house: and she shall shave her head, and pare her nails: And she shall put the rainment of her captivity from off her. And shall remain in thine house, and bewail her father and her mother a full month: and after that thou shall go in unto her and be her husband, and she shall be thy wife. And it shall be, if thou have no delight in her, then thou shalt let her go wither she will; buy thou shalt not sell her at all for money thou shall not make merchandise of her, because thou hast humbled her."* Since YisraEL only have one manner of law for the home born and the stranger that soujourneth with them, the set time to bewail or mourn was a full month, which is 30 days read:

Deuteronomy 34v8 *"And the children of YisraEL wept for Moses in the plains of Moab thirty days: So the days of weeping and mourning for Moses were ended."*

Numbers 20v28-29 *"And Moses stripped Aaron of his garments, and put them upon Eleazar his son; and Aaron died there in the top of the mount; and Moses and Eleazar came down from the mount. And when all the congregation saw that Aaron was dead, they mourned for Aaron thirty days, even all the house of Yisrael."*

__Genesis7v11-12__ *"In the six hundred year of Noah's life, in the second month, the seventh day of the month, the same day were all the fountains of the great deep broken up, and the windows of heaven were opened. And the rain was upon the earth forty days and forty nights.*

Genesis 8v1-4 *"And Elohim remembered Noah, and every living thing, and all the cattle that was with him in the ark: And Elohim made a wind to pass over the earth, and the waters asswaged; the fountains also of the deep and the windows of heaven were stopped, and the rain from heaven was restrained: and the waters returned from off the earth continually: and after the end of the hundred and fifty days the waters were abated. And the ark rested in the seventh month, on the seventeenth day of the month, upon the mountains of Ararat. And the waters decreased continually until the tenth month: in the tenth month, on the first day of the month, were the tops of the mountains."* The 2nd month through 7th month = 150 days = 5 months. There is no 28, 29, or 31 days in a month.

TWELVE MONTHS A YEAR

All over the Scriptures it is clear that the year is a set number of months, which is twelve. I will prove beyond a shadow of a doubt that a year is not what is commonly taught in the various synagogues or churches, that a year can be twelve or thirteen months.

In **I Chronicles 27** all of the months of the year were mentioned. This was during King David's 40-year reign.

I Chronicles 27v1 *"Now the children of YisraEL, after their number, to wit, the chief fathers and captains of thousands and hundreds, and their officers that served the king in any matter of the courses, which came in and went out month by month throughout all the months of the year, of every course were twenty and four thousand."*

I Kings 4v7 *"And Solomon had twelve officers over all YisraEL, which provided victuals for the King and his household: each man his month in a year."*

Daniel 12v28-33 *"All this came upon the king Nebuchadnezzar. At the end of twelve months he walked in the palace of the kingdom of Babylon. The king spake, and said, is not this great Babylon, that I have built for the house of the kingdom by the might of my power, and for the honour of my majesty? While the word was in the king's mouth, there fell a voice from heaven, saying, O king Nebuchadnezzar, to thee it is spoken; The kingdom is departed from thee. And they shall drive thee from men, and thy dwelling shall be with the beasts of the field: they shall make thee to eat grass as oxen and seven times shall pass over thee, until thou know that the Most High ruleth in the kingdom of men, and giveth it to whomsoever He will. The same hour was the thing fulfilled upon Nebuchadnezzar: and he was driven from men, and did eat grass as oxen, and his body was wet with the dew of heaven, till his hairs were grown like eagles' feathers, and his nails like birds' claws."*

From the book of Genesis through the book of Malachi every month of the year was mentioned at least two or more times; but there is no mention of a 13th month. Not one time as taught by some religious groups.

MONTHS OF THE YEAR IN THE SCRIPTURES

According to the Holy Scriptures all the months throughout the year were mentioned by their number. Although, many months are mentioned by name, the only month that was mentioned out of the mouth of YAHWEH by name, is the month of Abib. The following scriptures are examples of how many times the months are mentioned in the scriptures. Throughout the whole book of the Scriptures of Truth there was never mentioned, not one time about a 13th month, PERIOD.

1. **First month:** Genesis 8v13; Exodus 12v2; Exodus 12v18; Exodus 40v2; Leviticus 23v5; Esther 3v7.
2. **Second month:** Genesis 7v11; Genesis 8v14; Exodus 16v1; Numbers 1v1; Numbers 1v18; I Kings 6v1.
3. **Third month:** Exodus 19v1; I Chronicles 27v5; II Chronicles 15v10; II Chronicles 31v7; Esther 8v9; Ezekiel 31v1.
4. **Fourth month:** II Kings 25v3; I Chronicles 27v7; Jeremiah 39v2; Jeremiah 52v6; Ezekiel 1v1; Zechariah 8v19.
5. **Fifth month:** Numbers 33v38; II Kings 25v8; I Chronicles 27v8; Ezra 7v8; Jeremiah 1v3; Jeremiah 28v1.
6. **Sixth month:** I Chronicles 27v9; Ezekiel 8v1; Haggai 1v1; Haggai 1v15.
7. **Seventh month:** Genesis 8v4; Leviticus 16v29; Leviticus 23v24; I Kings 8v2; Numbers 29v12; I Chronicles 27v10.
8. **Eighth month:** I Kings 6v38; I Kings 12v32; I Chronicles 27v11; Zechariah 1v1.
9. **Ninth month:** Zechariah 7v1; Haggai 2v10; Jeremiah 36v22; Ezra 10v9; I Chronicles 27v13.
10. **Tenth month:** Genesis 8v5; Zechariah 8v19; Ezekiel 33v21; Ezra 10v16; I Chronicles 27v13
11. **Eleventh month:** Zechariah 9v7; I Chronicles 27v14; Deuteronomy 1v3.
12. **Twelfth month:** Ezekiel 32v1; Jeremiah 52v31; Esther 3v13; I Chronicles 27v15; II Kings 25v27.

SEVEN SABBATHS OF YEARS

According to the Holy Scriptures YAHWEH commanded we should number seven sabbath of years. It is very abundant in the Scriptures that numbering the years by seven was the custom of YisraEL as well as the patriarchs before them. Jacob served Laban seven years for his wife Leah and seven more years for his wife Rachael. Joseph revealed to Pharaoh the interpretation of his dream which was seven years of plenty followed by seven years of famine. Read:

Genesis 41v25-28 *"And Joseph said unto Pharaoh, the dream of Pharaoh is one: Elohim has shown Pharaoh what he is about to do. The seven good kine are seven years; and the seven good ears are seven years: the dream is one. And the seven thin and ill favoured kine that came up after them are seven years; and the seven empty ears blasted with the east wind shall be seven years of famine. This is the thing which I have spoken unto Pharaoh: What Elohim is about to do he sheweth unto Pharaoh."*

Leviticus 25v8-9 *"and thou shalt number Seven Sabbaths of Years unto thee; seven times seven years; and the space of the seven sabbaths of years shall be unto thee forty-nine years."*

Exodus23v10-11 *"And six years thou shall sow thy land, and gather in the fruits there of: but the seventh year thou shall let it rest and lie still; that the poor of thy people may eat; and what they leave the beasts of the field shall eat. In like manner thou shall deal with thy vineyard, and with thy olive yard."*

Deuteronomy 15v1 *"At the end of every seven years thou shalt make a release. And this is the manner of the release: Every creditor that lendeth ought unto his neighbor shall release it; he shall not exact it of his neighbor or of his brother; because it is called YAH's release."*

Deuteronomy 31v9-11 *"And Moses wrote this Law and delivered it unto the priests the sons of Levi, which bare the ark of the covenant of Yah and unto all the elders of YisraEL. And Moses commanded them, saying at the end of every seven years, in the solemnity of the year of release, in the feast of tabernacles, when all YisraEL is come to appear before Yah thy Elohim in the place which he shall choose, thou shalt read this law before all YisraEL in their hearing."*

It is clear that the years in the Scriptures are numbered in a cycle of seven. It is essential to understand these years to follow YAH Sabbath of Years.

Chapter 3

YAH'S Signs, Seasons, Days, & Years

YAHWEH Signs Seasons Days Years

FOREWORD

Many nations, religions, and organizations have made their own calendars using the signs of heavens as stated in the Holy Scriptures (Gen 1v14). I will prove beyond a shadow of any doubt that YAHWEH has his own calendar in the Scriptures that all the ancient Holy men followed, including the Children of YisraEL. I will prove YAHWEH Calendar by using actual scripture dates, real scripture events and actual ages of the Patriarch's. YAHWEH stated in the book of Amos 3v7 "Surely YAHWEH ELOHIM will do nothing, unless he reveals his secret to his servants the prophets." YAHWEH have always used his servants to fulfill his purposes or desires. According to the book of Isaiah 49v 3 YAHWEH stated "And he said to me, you are my servant, O YisraEL, in whom I will be glorified." Also YisraEL is said to be the only nation that YAH have known (read Amos 3v1-2). To understand the Signs, Seasons, Days, and Years used in the Scriptures one must accept simple truth declared in the Scriptures of Truth.

1. The first **date** given in the scriptures was during the time of Noah when YAHWEH destroyed the earth by flood. When this **date** was given it is crystal clear that YAHWEH established 30 days in each Month (read Gen 7v 1-24 and Gen 8v 1-22). The days of each month all through the scriptures only revealed 30 days (read Due 21v 10-14, Numb 20v 22-29, Due 34v 7-8).

2. The scriptures also revealed 12 months in the year. King David established 12 officers from each tribe that he personally named to serve the King month by month throughout all the months of the year (read 1st Chronicles 27v 1-15). King Solomon followed his father and personally named 12 Governors that served him one month of the year (read 1st Kings 4v 1-19).

3. YAHWEH also established that his years were counted by seven called the **Sabbath of Years**, with the seventh year being a Sabbath for the land, a Sabbath to YAH in Leviticus 25v 8 " And you shall count seven **Sabbaths of Years** for yourself, seven times seven years; and the time of the seven **Sabbaths of Years** shall be to you 49 years". (Also read Exodus 23v 10-11, Leviticus 25v 1-7, and Leviticus 25v 20-22).

When sincerely considering these three factors, one will come to the undeniable truth, the calendar that YAH created and used in the scriptures is diverse from all the calendars used todayt is also a truth that when using YAHWEH Signs, Seasons, Days, and Years one can use this for the past, present, and future events including the correct time for the holy days, prophecies, and ages of the Patriarch's. I will provide seven different charts including other information to detail the truth. This information is only for the total and **exclusive exaltation** of the Most High.

By Mowreh IshiYAH YIsraEL   House of YisraEL North Carolina   Phone: (919) 931-6216

YAHWEH Signs Seasons Days Years

YAHWEH SABBATH OF YEARS

According to the Holy Scriptures YAHWEH has appointed times in his Sabbath of Years. By knowing the appointed times you will gain a better understanding of YAHWEH years. YAHWEH counts his years by seven. The appointed years of YAH are not feasts.

1) **Third Year:** this year is called the year of tithing. (Deuteronomy 26v12-19) Although tithing was done every year, at the end of the third year tithes were set aside for the Levite, stranger, fatherless, and the widow in the gates where the people lived instead of being brought to Jerusalem. (Deuteronomy 14v28). This is only done in the third year.
2) **Sixth Year:** this year is called the year that YAH commanded his blessing. YAHWEH proclaimed the seventh year, a Sabbath for the land, a Sabbath to YAH, so in the sixth year he said he would command his blessing and bring forth fruit for three years. (Leviticus 25v20-22) This is only done in the sixth year.
3) **Sabbath of Years:** the seventh year was called the Sabbath for the Land. The Children of YisraEL was commanded to sow there field and prune there vine yard for six years but in the Seventh year shall be a Sabbath of rest unto the land, a Sabbath for YAH. This is only done in the Seventh Year. (Leviticus 25v1-2)
4) **Year of Release:** The Year of Release was also in the Seventh year but specifically at the End of the Seventh Year. At the end of this year every creditor that lendeth unto his neighbor shall release it. He shall not exact it of his neighbor, or his brother, it is YAH's release, of a foreigner it can be exacted (Deuteronomy 15v1-3) this is only done at the end of the seventh year.
5) **Year of Reading Law:** The reading of Law took place in the Seventh year, at the end of the year, in the feast of Tabernacles. Moses commanded the people that every seven years, in the solemnity of the year of release, in the feast of Tabernacles, when all YisraEL come to appear before YAH in the place he shall choose, thou shall read the law before all YisraEL in their hearing. (Deuteronomy31v9-11) This is only done in the seventh year at the feast of tabernacles.
6) **Year of Trumpet of Jubilee Sound:** The trumpet of Jubilee was sounded every 49th year, which is the Seventh Sabbath of Years. The trumpet was sounded at the end of the year in the Day of Atonement. The trumpet sound represented freedom for the 50th year. (Leviticus 25v8-9) This is only done in the Seventh Sabbath of Years on the Day of Atonement
7) **Year of Jubilee:** The Jubilee was the 50th year. A proclamation of liberty was made through out all the land for the inhabitants. In this 50th year there was no sowing or reaping. The land laid fallow for the poor, and the beast of the field. The vineyard and the olive grove also. (Exodus 23v 10-11) This is only done the Fiftieth Year.

By Mowreh IshiYAH YIsraEL   House of YisraEL North Carolina   Phone: (919) 931-6216

YAHWEH Signs Seasons Days Years

430 years in Egypt

    According to the book Genesis 41v1-36 Pharaoh had a dream at the End of two years (SECOND YEAR). This was preceded by the feast pharaoh had on his birthday where he restored the butler to his position and hung the baker as Joseph revealed in their dreams while in prison. According to the scriptures Genesis 40v20-23 Pharaoh's birthday was on the third day, the third day is the new moon of the third year of YAH Sabbath of years. The first dream of Pharaoh was about seven fat fine looking cows being eaten by seven ugly and gaunt cows, the horror of the dream woke him up. Pharaoh had a second dream about seven plump, good heads of grain in one stalk being devoured by seven thin heads, this nightmare also awoke him. The dream revealed was seven years of plenty followed by seven years of famine. The dream was repeated to Pharaoh twice because the thing was established by Elohim and he would shortly bring it to pass. The famine would be so severe that Joseph stated the famine would make the years of plenty be forgotten.

    *Since the dream came at the end of the 2nd year (Remember YAH years are counted by seven) 3rd-4th year = 1st year plenty, 4th-5th year=2nd year of plenty, 5th-6th year= 3rd year of plenty, 6th-7th year= 4th year of plenty, 7th-1st year = 5th year of plenty, 1st-2nd year = 6th year of plenty, and the 2nd-3rd year= 7th year of plenty; seven years of plenty. Following these years are the years of famine. 3rd -4th year = 1st year of famine, 4th-5th= 2nd year of famine. **According to Genesis 45v1-11 Joseph revealed himself to his brothers and charged them to bring their family and his father to Egypt so they would not fall to poverty and die in the Second year of the famine, and that there were five years of famine remaining. The Children of YisraEL walked down into Egypt the Second Year of the Famine which was the <u>5th year of YAH Sabbath of years</u>.** According to Exodus 12v40-42 the Children of YisraEL sojourned in Egypt 430 years. <u>When counting by YAH Sabbath of years(1-7 years)</u> 430 years from the 5th year, the Second year of the famine the Children of YisraEL sojourned Exactly 430 years as YAH stated and they departed in the 1st month, 1st year, of the 15th day of the month. The chart 430 years in Egypt illustrates the years of plenty, famine, and the sojourning of the Children of YisraEL. <u>This truth can only be proven by counting by YAH's Sabbaths of Years.</u>*

NOTE: *When counting 30 days a month, 12 months a year, the third year begins on the third day of the week*

By Mowreh IshiYAH YIsraEL   House of YisraEL North Carolina   Phone: (919) 931-6216

YAHWEH Signs Seasons Days Years

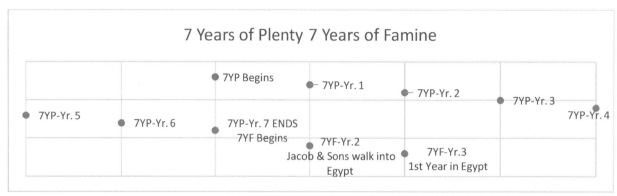

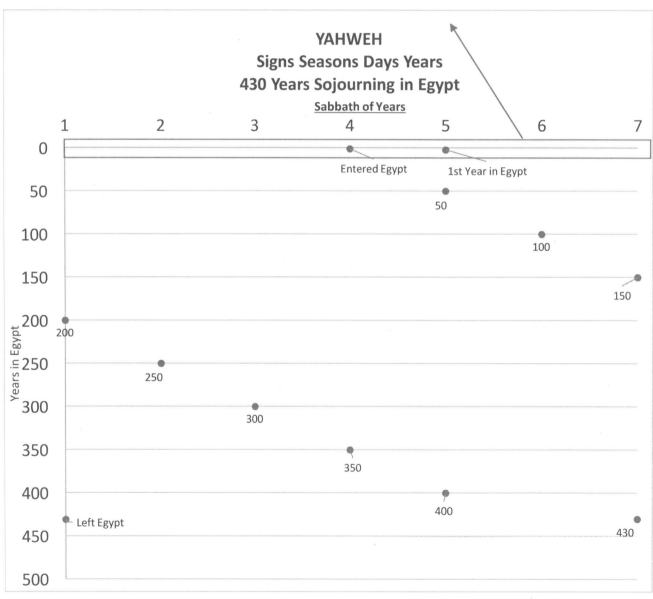

By Mowreh IshiYAH YIsraEL   House of YisraEL North Carolina   Phone: (919) 931-6216

YAHWEH Signs Seasons Days Years

480 Years after Leaving Egypt the Foundation of the Temple Built

According to 1KINGS 6V 1-37, King Solomon began to build the foundation of the House of YAH 480 years after the Children of YisraEL had come out of Egypt in the fourth year of his reign. In the second month of this fourth year the foundation of the House of YAH was laid. In the eleventh year the eighth month the house of YAH was finished in all its details according to its plans. Solomon took seven years to build the House of YAH. As previously stated YAH's years are counted by seven. ***After counting by seven from the first year coming out of Egypt, 480 years later you will fall exactly in the 4th year as the scriptures state (I King 6v37). The chart 480 Years after Leaving Egypt the Foundation of the Temple was built, illustrates the 1st year through 480 years later, is the fourth year of King Solomon and the fourth year of YAH Sabbath of years. This truth can only be proven by using YAH's Sabbaths of Years (1-7 years).***

By Mowreh IshiYAH YIsraEL   House of YisraEL North Carolina   Phone: (919) 931-6216

YAHWEH Signs Seasons Days Years

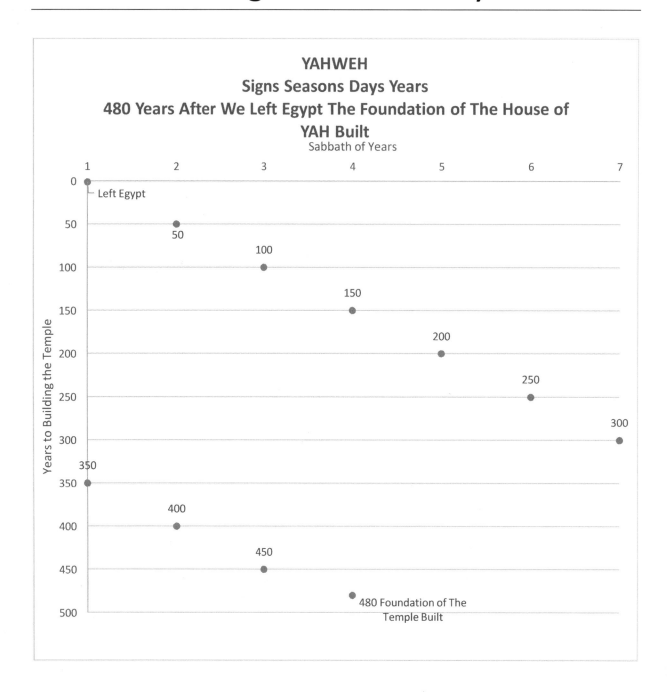

YAHWEH Signs Seasons Days Years

40 Years in the Wilderness & 40 Years Eating Manna

According to the Holy Scriptures YAHWEH stated the Children of YisraEL would sojourn in the wilderness for 40 years, they also would eat manna for 40 years. (Read Deuteronomy 8v1-17, Exodus 16v35) The Children of YisraEL departed Egypt on the 15th of the 1st month of the 1st year at night. (Read Deuteronomy 16v1, Numbers 33v3) The first day in the wilderness was the morning of the 16th of the 1st month in the 1st year (Read Exodus 14v24-30). 40 years later they came to a place they called Gilgal, where they kept the Passover. The day after the Passover they ate the produce of the Land of Canaan. The day after they ate the produce of the land of Canaan the Manna ceased. Since the Passover is on the 14th they ate the produce of the land on the 15th, the Manna ceased on the 16th, exactly 40 years later. Also they were officially out of the wilderness on the 16th because they encamped at the walls of Jericho (Read Joshua 5v10-15). *As illustrated in the chart 40 years in the Wilderness and 40 Years Eating Manna the Children of YisraEL came in the Wilderness on the 16th day and they came to a land inhabited on the 16th as YAHWEH stated, exactly 40 years (Exodus 16v35). <u>This truth can only be proven by using YAH's Sabbath of Years (1-7 years).</u>*

YAHWEH Signs Seasons Days Years

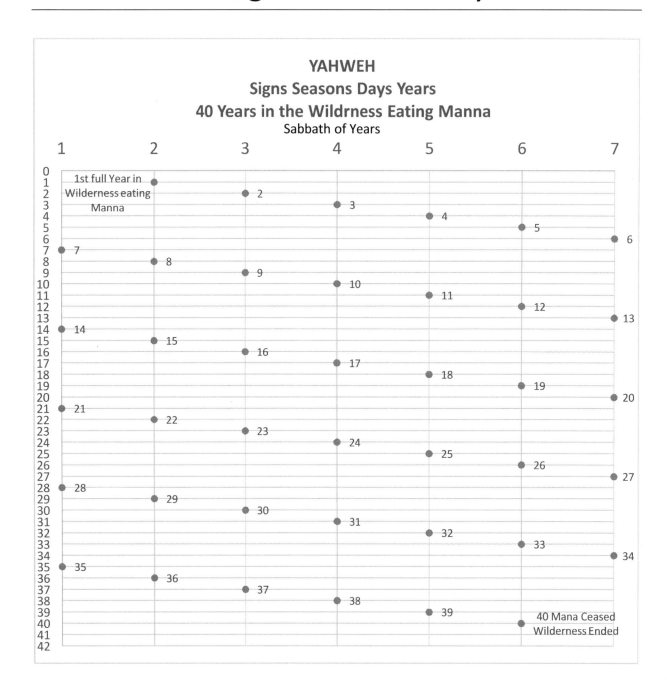

By Mowreh IshiYAH YIsraEL   House of YisraEL North Carolina   Phone: (919) 931-6216

YAHWEH Signs Seasons Days Years

The Life of Moses

According to the Book of Exodus 7v6 Moses stood before Pharaoh when he was 80 years old. When Moses spoke the words "I am one hundred and twenty years old today, I can no longer go out and come in" (Deuteronomy 1v3), It was the Eleventh month of the 40th year, which probably was his birth month (read Deuteronomy 31v1-2). 80 years + 40 years= 120 years. Since Moses seemed to turn 80 in the eleventh month and the Children of YisraEL left Egypt in the 1st month, 15th day (Exodus 12v1-2, Numbers 33v3), YAH performed his miracles and wonders before pharaoh in Egypt in a matter of weeks. **Also since they departed Egypt in the 1st year, Moses had to speak to Pharaoh in the 7th year.** *As illustrated in the chart the life of Moses, he was 80 years old in Egypt and lived 40 years exactly in the wilderness.*

By Mowreh IshiYAH YIsraEL   House of YisraEL North Carolina   Phone: (919) 931-6216

YAHWEH Signs Seasons Days Years

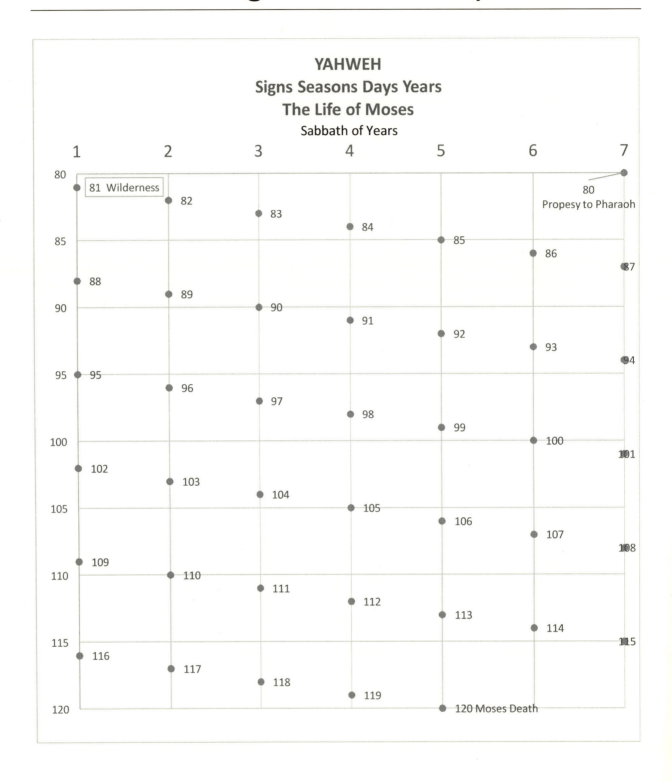

By Mowreh IshiYAH YIsraEL   House of YisraEL North Carolina   Phone: (919) 931-6216

YAHWEH Signs Seasons Days Years

Caleb Establishes the Land of YAHUDAH

According to the Holy Scriptures Caleb was one of two men who was above 20 years old whom YAHWEH allowed to enter he promise land because he had another spirit (Read Numbers 14v20-25, Numbers 14v29-31). Caleb was 40 years old when he entered the Wilderness for he said YAHWEH kept him alive 45 more years when he took the land known today as the land of Yahudah, he was from that tribe, and he was 85 years old (Read Joshua 14v6-15). Caleb was one of the 12 men selected to spy out the land of Canaan. (Read Number 13v1-16). Moses instructed the men to bring back some fruit of the land and since it was the time of the season of the first ripe grapes, the 12 men likely spied the land in the first year of the Wilderness at the End of the Year in the Seventh month (Read Numbers 13v17-20, Exodus 23v14-16). **When counting by seven** *as illustrated in the chart Caleb Establishes the Land of Yahudah when he turned 85 years old, the land of Yahudah was established in the 4th year of YAH'S Sabbath of Years.*

YAHWEH Signs Seasons Days Years

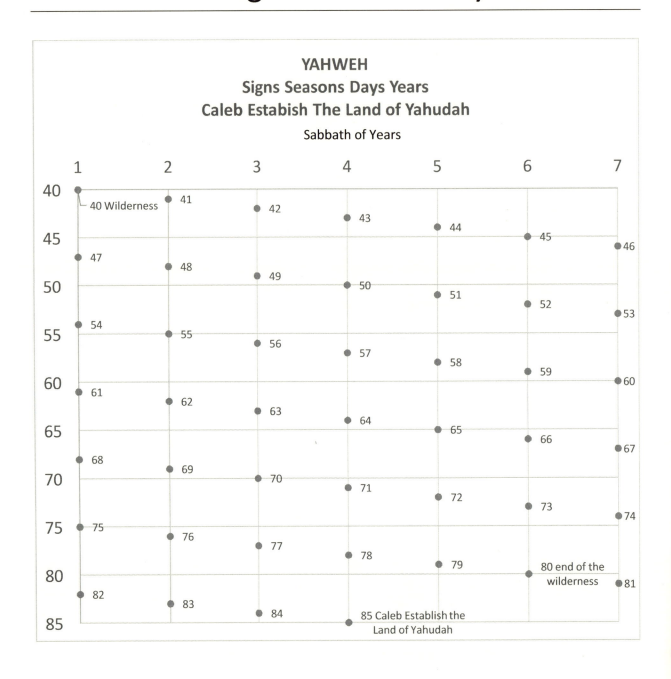

By Mowreh IshiYAH YIsraEL   House of YisraEL North Carolina   Phone: (919) 931-6216

YAHWEH Signs Seasons Days Years

Book of the Genealogy of Adam

According to the Holy Scriptures Adam was created on the sixth day, which was 2 days after YAH made the luminaries in heaven, for signs, seasons, days and years; Adam was created the second day after the 1st moon, the 1st season, in the 1st year. By numbering every seven years, which is YAH method of counting the years, you can only come to the undeniable truth, that YAH has his own Signs, Seasons, Days, and Years that the patriarch's used including the Children of YisraEL. The following seven points will prove YAH's method of counting establishes the truth.

1) According to the Holy Scriptures Noah was 500 years old when he began to have sons. (Genesis 5v32) Japheth was born in the 500th year of Noah because he was the elder son. (Genesis 10:2) Also read (Genesis 10v1-5) this was the 2nd year of YAH's Sabbaths of Years. Also refer to the chart *The Book of the Genealogy of Adam*

2) Ham was the second son born to Noah in the 501st year of his life (Genesis 10v1-20) Also two of the rivers that parted from the river that watered the garden of Eden compassed Ham's sons Havilah and Cush. (Genesis 2v10-14. This was the 3rd year of YAH's Sabbaths of Years.

3) Shem was the third son born to Noah in the 502nd year of his life. (Genesis 10v1-32) Shem was 100 years old when he begat Arphaxad 2 years after the flood. (Genesis 11v10) The flood was in the 600th year of Noah's life, and 2 years after this, the 602nd year of Noah life, Arphaxad was born and Shem was exactly 100 years old. This was the 4th year of YAH's Sabbaths of Years.

4) When Joseph was made ruler to stand before Pharaoh King of Egypt he was 30 years old. This was the beginning of the seven years of plenty and the 3rd year of YAH's Sabbaths of Years (Read Genesis 41v46-56) Also refer to the chart *The Book of the Genealogy of Adam*

5) When Joseph revealed his self to his brothers and charged them to go and get their father and bring all they have into Egypt so they would not fall into poverty and die it was the 2nd year of the Famine, this was the 5th year of YAH's Sabbaths of Years. (Read Genesis 45v1-11) Also refer to the chart *The Book of the Genealogy of Adam*

6) When Jacob enters Egypt in the end of the 2nd year of the famine, with 5 years of famine remaining, this was the 4th year of YAH's Sabbaths of Years. Also refer to the chart *The Book of the Genealogy of Adam*

7) When Most High divided the inheritance to the nations and separated the sons of Adam, he set boundaries of the people according to the number of the Children of YisraEL (Read Deuteronomy 32v8-9). Also refer to the chart The Book of the Genealogy of Adam.

Adam Sons: 1. Seth 2. Enos 3. Cainan 4. Mahalaleel 5. Jared 6. Enoch 7. Methuselah 8. Lamech 9. Noah 10. Japheth 11. Ham 12. Shem (Genesis 5v1-32)

By Mowreh IshiYAH YIsraEL   House of YisraEL North Carolina   Phone: (919) 931-6216

YAHWEH Signs Seasons Days Years

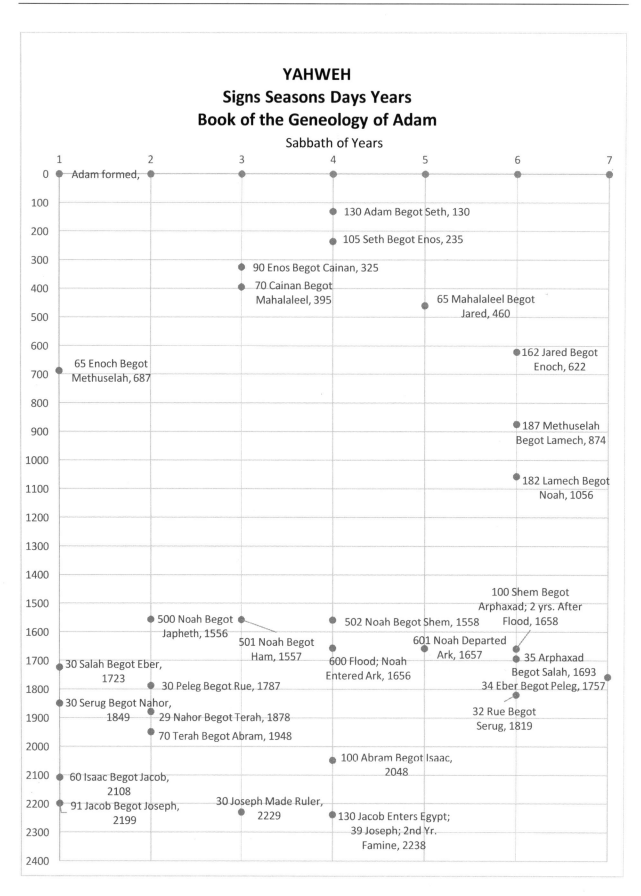

Chapter 4

YAH'S Secret Signs and the Timeline of the Scriptures

Including the Reference Section:
1. Special Months
    1. Abib
    2. The Third Month
    3. The Fourth Month
    4. The Year of Tithing
2. Seven Year Calendar snapshot

3. YAH'S Set Times wall Calendar 1st Year.

Mowreh IshiYAH YisraEL 1
House of YisraEL of Raleigh, NC

YAHWEH'S Secret Signs
&
Timeline of the Scriptures

By Mowreh IshiYAH Ben YisraEL of the House of YisraEL of Raleigh, NC

Is. 42:21:
YAHWEH is well pleased for his righteousness sake he will magnify the law and make it honorable.

According to the Holy Scriptures YAH left a timeline of major events. These events provide for us various dates of days, months, and years. When examining this timeline very closely you will discover one of YAH'S secret signs. His timeline also will prove beyond a shadow of a doubt that YAH signs, seasons, days, and years are diverse from all the other calendars used today, that the patriarchs and the children of YisraEL followed.

1st Year: Gen 1:14-19

1st Month: According to the book of Genesis, the lights were made on the fourth day for signs, seasons, days, and years. Three days after the lights were made, YAH called the seventh day a Sabbath to YAH. This Sabbath came three days after the very first Sun, Moon, and Stars. This can only mean that the Sabbaths of the first month are the 3rd, 10th, 17th, and 24th day of the month.

2nd Month: Exodus 16:1-24: The Children of YisraEL came to the wilderness of Sin on the 15th day of the 2nd month, after departing the land of Egypt. The Children of YisraEL complained about needing bread, so, YAH gave them quails in the evening of the 15th and the next morning he provided bread from heaven. He commanded them to gather this bread from heaven for six days and on the sixth day he will give them twice as much for some to be left until the next morning, because the seventh day will be a Sabbath to YAH. On the seventh day he told the people that there won't be any in the field. Since the bread came the morning after the 15th, seven days later, it could only mean that the 7th day was on the 22nd of the 2nd month. The Sabbaths for the second month are the 1st, 8th, 15th, 22nd, and 29th of the month.

3rd Month: Exodus 19:1-10 & Exodus 24:12-18: The children of YisraEL came to the wilderness of Sinai on the very first day of the third month which was the first day of the week. The last day of the second month was the 29th, which is on the Sabbath. They were commanded to be ready on the third day of the week. For in this third day YAH would come down on Mt Sinai to make a covenant with the people.

Exodus 24:12-18: YAH came down on the third day, onto Mt. Sinai and spoke the Ten Commandments to the Children of YisraEL and called Moses from the cloud. They were on the mountain for six days then Moses went into the cloud on the seventh day, to receive the Ten Commandments. The Sabbaths of the third month are the 6th, 13th, 20th, and 27th. When following this timeline of the first year you will see that there are 30 days every month, all the way up to the third month of the first year.

3rd Year: Genesis 40:8-23 & Genesis 41:1

Yoseph was falsely accused of committing a crime in Egypt and was placed in the custody of the captain of the guard. While there he interpreted the dreams of the chief butler and the chief baker, who were also detained. The dream came to pass after three days, which was the third day on Pharaoh's birthday, at the end of two full years. When counting from the first month, 30 days each month, 12 months in the year, at end of two full years the third year begins on the third day.

Year of Tithing: **Deuteronomy 26:12-19**: The Children of YisraEL were commanded to bring all the tithes of the third year and lay it up in their gates or cities for the Levites, the widow, the fatherless, and the stranger at the end of that year. The end of this third year is the Seventh month. When counting 30 days each month and 12 months in the year you will discover that this year of tithing coincides with the same month that YAH made a covenant with YisraEL on Mount Sinai. The Sabbaths of the seventh month are the 6th, 13th, 20th, 27th.

4th Year, 2nd Month, 2nd Day: 1st Kings 6:1-37

480 years after the children of YisraEL came out of the land of Egypt, in the 4th Year of Solomon's reign over YisraEL, in the second month, Solomon began to build the House of YAH. When counting from the first month, 30 days in each month, 12 months each year, 480 years later, is exactly the fourth year of Solomon. The second month of this fourth year when the temple was being built coincides with the same month that YAH came down on Mt Sinai and made a covenant with the Children of YisraEL. The Sabbaths of this month are the 6th, 13th, 20th, and 27th.

4th Year, 2nd Month, 2nd Day: Genesis 7 & 8:

In the 600th year of Noah, YAH destroyed the earth by floodwaters. Noah, his sons, and their wives were commanded to get in the ark on the 600th year, in the second month. When counting from the first month with 30 days in each month, 12 months in each year, which is 1,656 years from Adam, the 600th year of Noah is the 4th year of YAH'S Sabbath of Years. This second month is the same month that coincides with the month that YAH came down on Mt Sinai and made a covenant with the Children of YisraEL. The Sabbaths of this month are 6th, 13th, 20th, and 27th.

5th year: Deut 1:1-8:

After sojourning in the wilderness 40 years, in the 11th month of this year YAH told the Children of YisraEL that they have dwelt long enough in this mountain. So, they began their journeys from that mount to the promised land in the 40th year in the 11th month. When counting 30 days each month, 12 months each year, this fortieth year becomes the fifth year of YAH's Sabbath of years. And the 11th month of this year coincides with the same Month that YAH made a covenant with the children of YisraEL on Mt. Sinai. Again, the Sabbaths of this month are the 6th, 13th, 20th, and 27th.

7th Year: Leviticus 25:1-10 and Exodus 23:10-11:

YAH commanded the Children of YisraEL to count seven Sabbaths of Years, the 7th Sabbath of years 7 times 7years, is the 49th year. In each seventh year the land was to rest in a Sabbath to YAH. When counting from the first month 30 days each month and 12 months each year the seventh Year begins on the first day of the week, which coincides with the same month when YAH made a covenant with the Children of YisraEL on Mt. Sinai.

After the 7th year, the first year will return back as it started to number another Sabbath year, until seven Sabbaths are complete.

7th Year, 2nd Day of the Month: Ezra 7:1-10 Ezra 8:15-23:

Ezra a skilled and expert scribe in the law of YAH was charged with overseeing the rebuilding of the temple of YAH coming out of the 70-year captivity of Babylon. Ezra departed from Babylon on the first day of the first month in the seventh year. He camped at the river of Ahava on the third day of this month, to seek YAH with fasting and prayer. YAH was entreated by them and blessed their journeys. As reported previously the seventh month the first day of this month coincides with the same month YAH made a covenant with the Children of YisraEL on Mount Sinai.

This timeline is provided with scriptures that any sincere individual can read and study to verify this truth. I also provided the calendar of YAH that, in its fullness, comes directly from the Holy Scriptures.

Abib
The First Month of the First Year

And Elohim said, Let there be lights in the firmament of the heaven to divide the day from the night; and let them be for signs, and for seasons, and for days, and years:

The Season YAH brought YisraEL out of the land of Egypt

YAH spake unto Moses and Aaron in the land of Egypt, saying, This month shall be unto you the beginning of months: it shall be the first month of the year to you.

Yom Echad	Yom Sheniy	Yom Shliyshiy	Yom Rbiy'iy	Yom Chamiyshiy	Yom Shishshiy	Yom Shabbat
The Day YAH Created Light Gen. 1:1-5 Day One	The Day YAH Created the Heavens Gen. 1:6-8 Day Two-2	The Day YAH Created the Sea, Earth, Grass, Herbs, and Trees Gen. 1:9-13 Day Three -2	The Day YAH Created the Lights Gen. 1:14-19 <u>Day of the 1st Month</u> Day Four -4	1 The Day YAH Created sea creatures and Fowls of the Air Gen 1:20-23 Day Five 1	2 The Day YAH created creeping things, beast, and Man on Earth Gen 1:24-31 Day Six	3 The Day YAH ceased from his work and sanctified this day; the First Sabbath Day: Gen. 2:1-3 **Day Seven**
4	5	6	7	8	9	10
11	12	13	14 **Passover/Pesach**	15 **Chag Matzo/ Feast of Unleavened Bread Day 1**	16 Day 2	17 Day 3
18 Day 4	19 Day 5	20 Day 6	21 Day 7	22	23	24
25	26	27	28	29		

שְׁלִישִׁי חֹדֶשׁ

The Third Month of the First Year

Turn, O backsliding children, saith YAH; for I am married unto you!

YAH is Married To YisraEL

Thus Saith YAH...

Ye have seen what I did unto the Egyptians, and how I bare you on eagles' wings, and brought you unto myself. Now therefore, if ye will obey my voice indeed, and keep my covenant, then ye shall be a peculiar treasure unto me above all people: for all the earth is mine: And ye shall be unto me a kingdom of priests, and an holy nation. These are the words which thou shalt speak unto the children of Yisrael. Ex. 19:4-5

Yom Echad	Yom Sheniy	Yom Shliyshiy	Yom Rbiy'iy	Yom Chamiyshiy	Yom Shishshiy	Yom Shabbat
Day of the 3rd Month Exodus 19:1	1	2 The Day YAH Spoke to YisraEL out of Heaven and made a Covenant With YisraEL Exodus 19:1-10	3	4	5	6 Moshe went to receive the 10 Commandments Exodus 24
7	8	9	10	11	12	13
14	15	16	17	18	19	20
21	22	23	24	25	26	27
28	29					

Deut. 4:12-13 And YAH spake unto you out of the midst of the fire: ye heard the voice of the words, but saw no similitude; only y heard a voice. And he declared unto you his covenant, which he commanded you to perform, even Ten Commandments; and he wrote th* upon two tables of stone.*

The Second month of the Fourth Year

I have chosen Jerusalem, that my name might be there; and have chosen David to be over my people Yisrael.

YAHWEH'S Holy Temple

Now mine eyes shall be open, and mine ears attend unto the prayer that is made in this place. For now have I chosen and sanctified this house, that my name may be there forever: and mine eyes and mine heart shall be there perpetually.

Yom Echad	Yom Sheniy	Yom Shliyshiy	Yom Rbiy'iy	Yom Chamiyshiy	Yom Shishshiy	Yom Shabbat
Day of the 2nd Month	1	2 The Day YAH'S House is built 480 Years Since YisraEL Left Egypt 1Kings 6:1 & II Chron 3:1-2	3	4	5	6
7	8	9	10	11	12	13
14	15	16	17 The Day YAH brought the Flood waters Gen 7:11	18	19	20
21	22	23	24	25	26	27
28	29					

The Seventh Month of the Third Year
Return unto me, and I will return unto you, saith YAH of hosts
The Year of Tithing

Then thou shalt say before YAH thy Elohim, I have brought away the hallowed things out of mine house...

Bring ye all the tithes into the storehouse, that there may be meat in mine house, and prove me now herewith, saith YAHWEH of hosts, if I will not open you the windows of heaven, and pour you out a blessing, that there shall not be room enough to receive it. Mal. 3:10

Yom Echad	Yom Sheniy	Yom Shliyshiy	Yom Rbiy'iy	Yom Chamiyshiy	Yom Shishshiy	Yom Shabbat
Day of the 7th Month Year of Tithing	1 **YOM Teruah**	2	3	4	5	6
7	8	9 **Fast of YOM Kippur Begins at Even**	10 **YOM KIPPUR**	11	12	13
14	15 **Chag Succoth Day 1**	16 Day 2	17 Day 3	18 Day 4	19 Day 5	20 Day 6
21 Day 7	22 **Shabbat of Solemnity**	23	24	25	26	27
28	29					

Deut. 26: 18 And YAHWEH hath avouched thee this day to be his peculiar people, as he hath promised thee, and that thou shoulde keep all his commandments;

Year 1

Month 1

Sun	Mon	Tue	Wed	Thu	Fri	Sat
			NM	1	2	3
4	5	6	7	8	9	10
11	12	13	14 PO	15 ULB	16	17
18	19	20	21 End ULB	22	23	24
25	26	27	28	29		

Month 2

Sun	Mon	Tue	Wed	Thu	Fri	Sat
					NM	1
2	3	4	5	6	7	8
9	10	11	12	13	14	15
16	17	18	19	20	21	22
23	24	25	26	27	28	29

Month 3

Sun	Mon	Tue	Wed	Thu	Fri	Sat
NM	1	2	3	4	5	6
7	8	9	10	11	12	13
14	15	16	17	18	19	20
21	22	23	24	25	26	27
28	29					

Month 4

Sun	Mon	Tue	Wed	Thu	Fri	Sat
		NM	1	2	3	4
5	6	7	8	9	10	11
12	13	14	15	16	17	18
19	20	21	22	23	24	25
26	27	28	29			

Month 5

Sun	Mon	Tue	Wed	Thu	Fri	Sat
				NM	1	2
3	4	5	6	7	8	9
10	11	12	13	14	15	16
17	18	19	20	21	22	23
24	25	26	27	28	29	

Month 6

Sun	Mon	Tue	Wed	Thu	Fri	Sat
1	2	3	4	5	6	7
8	9	10	11	12	13	14
15	16	17	18	19	20	21
22	23	24	25	26	27	28
29						

Month 7

Sun	Mon	Tue	Wed	Thu	Fri	Sat
	NM BT	1	2	3	4	5
6	7	8	9 EVE DA	10 DA	11	12
13	14	15 FT	16	17	18	19
20	21	22	23	24	25	26
27	28	29				

Month 8

Sun	Mon	Tue	Wed	Thu	Fri	Sat
						3
4	5	6	7	8	9	10
11	12	13	14	15	16	17
18	19	20	21	22	23	24
25	26	27	28	29		

Month 9

Sun	Mon	Tue	Wed	Thu	Fri	Sat
2	3	4	5	6	7	8
9	10	11	12	13	14	15
16	17	18	19	20	21	22
23	24	25	26	27	28	29

Month 10

Sun	Mon	Tue	Wed	Thu	Fri	Sat
	1	2	3	4	5	6
7	8	9	10	11	12	13
14	15	16	17	18	19	20
21	22	23	24	25	26	27
28	29					

Month 11

Sun	Mon	Tue	Wed	Thu	Fri	Sat
		NM	1	2	3	4
5	6	7	8	9	10	11
12	13	14	15	16	17	18
19	20	21	22	23	24	25
26	27	28	29			

Month 12

Sun	Mon	Tue	Wed	Thu	Fri	Sat
				NM	1	2
3	4	5	6	7	8	9
10	11	12	13	14	15	16
17	18	19	20	21	22	23
24	25	26	27	28	29	

By Mowreh IshiYAH YisraEL 2014

Year 2

Month 1

Sun	Mon	Tue	Wed	Thu	Fri	Sat
						NM
1	2	3	4	5	6	7
8	9	10	11	12	13	14
15	16	17	18	19	20	21
22	23	24	25	26	27	28
29						

Month 2

Sun	Mon	Tue	Wed	Thu	Fri	Sat
	NM	1	2	3	4	5
6	7	8	9	10	11	12
13	14	15	16	17	18	19
20	21	22	23	24	25	26
27	28	29				

Month 3

Sun	Mon	Tue	Wed	Thu	Fri	Sat
			NM	1	2	3
4	5	6	7	8	9	10
11	12	13	14	15	16	17
18	19	20	21	22	23	24
25	26	27	28	29		

Month 4

Sun	Mon	Tue	Wed	Thu	Fri	Sat
					NM	1
2	3	4	5	6	7	8
9	10	11	12	13	14	15
16	17	18	19	20	21	22
23	24	25	26	27	28	29

Month 5

Sun	Mon	Tue	Wed	Thu	Fri	Sat
NM	1	2	3	4	5	6
7	8	9	10	11	12	13
14	15	16	17	18	19	20
21	22	23	24	25	26	27
28	29					

Month 6

Sun	Mon	Tue	Wed	Thu	Fri	Sat
		NM	1	2	3	4
5	6	7	8	9	10	11
12	13	14	15	16	17	18
19	20	21	22	23	24	25
26	27	28	29			

Month 7

Sun	Mon	Tue	Wed	Thu	Fri	Sat
				NM	1	2
3	4	5	6	7	8	9
10	11	12	13	14	15	16
17	18	19	20	21	22	23
24	25	26	27	28	29	

Month 8

Sun	Mon	Tue	Wed	Thu	Fri	Sat
						NM
1	2	3	4	5	6	7
8	9	10	11	12	13	14
15	16	17	18	19	20	21
22	23	24	25	26	27	28

Month 9

Sun	Mon	Tue	Wed	Thu	Fri	Sat
	NM	1	2	3	4	5
6	7	8	9	10	11	12
13	14	15	16	17	18	19
20	21	22	23	24	25	26
27	28	29				

Month 10

Sun	Mon	Tue	Wed	Thu	Fri	Sat
			NM	1	2	3
4	5	6	7	8	9	10
11	12	13	14	15	16	17
18	19	20	21	22	23	24
25	26	27	28	29		

Month 11

Sun	Mon	Tue	Wed	Thu	Fri	Sat
					NM	1
2	3	4	5	6	7	8
9	10	11	12	13	14	15
16	17	18	19	20	21	22
23	24	25	26	27	28	29

Month 12

Sun	Mon	Tue	Wed	Thu	Fri	Sat
NM	1	2	3	4	5	6
7	8	9	10	11	12	13
14	15	16	17	18	19	20
21	22	23	24	25	26	27
28	29					

Year 3

Month 1

Sun	Mon	Tue	Wed	Thu	Fri	Sat
		NM	1	2	3	4
5	6	7	8	9	10	11
12	13	14	15	16	17	18
19	20	21	22	23	24	25
26	27	28	29			

Month 2

Sun	Mon	Tue	Wed	Thu	Fri	Sat
				NM	1	2
3	4	5	6	7	8	9
10	11	12	13	14	15	16
17	18	19	20	21	22	23
24	25	26	27	28	29	

Month 3

Sun	Mon	Tue	Wed	Thu	Fri	Sat
						NM
1	2	3	4	5	6	7
8	9	10	11	12	13	14
15	16	17	18	19	20	21
22	23	24	25	26	27	28
29						

Month 4

Sun	Mon	Tue	Wed	Thu	Fri	Sat
	NM	1	2	3	4	5
6	7	8	9	10	11	12
13	14	15	16	17	18	19
20	21	22	23	24	25	26
27	28	29				

Month 5

Sun	Mon	Tue	Wed	Thu	Fri	Sat
			NM	1	2	3
4	5	6	7	8	9	10
11	12	13	14	15	16	17
18	19	20	21	22	23	24
25	26	27	28	29		

Month 6

Sun	Mon	Tue	Wed	Thu	Fri	Sat
					NM	1
2	3	4	5	6	7	8
9	10	11	12	13	14	15
16	17	18	19	20	21	22
23	24	25	26	27	28	29

Month 7

Sun	Mon	Tue	Wed	Thu	Fri	Sat
NM	1	2	3	4	5	6
7	8	9	10	11	12	13
14	15	16	17	18	19	20
21	22	23	24	25	26	27
28	29					

Month 8

Sun	Mon	Tue	Wed	Thu	Fri	Sat
		NM	1	2	3	4
5	6	7	8	9	10	11
12	13	14	15	16	17	18
19	20	21	22	23	24	25
26	27	28	29			

Month 9

Sun	Mon	Tue	Wed	Thu	Fri	Sat
				NM	1	2
3	4	5	6	7	8	9
10	11	12	13	14	15	16
17	18	19	20	21	22	23
24	25	26	27	28	29	

Month 10

Sun	Mon	Tue	Wed	Thu	Fri	Sat
						NM
1	2	3	4	5	6	7
8	9	10	11	12	13	14
15	16	17	18	19	20	21
22	23	24	25	26	27	28
29						

Month 11

Sun	Mon	Tue	Wed	Thu	Fri	Sat
	NM	1	2	3	4	5
6	7	8	9	10	11	12
13	14	15	16	17	18	19
20	21	22	23	24	25	26
27	28	29				

Month 12

Sun	Mon	Tue	Wed	Thu	Fri	Sat
			NM	1	2	3
4	5	6	7	8	9	10
11	12	13	14	15	16	17
18	19	20	21	22	23	24
25	26					

By Mowreh IshiYAH YisraEL 2014

Year 4

Month 1

Sun	Mon	Tue	Wed	Thu	Fri	Sat
					NM	1
2	3	4	5	6	7	8
9	10	11	12	13	14	15
16	17	18	19	20	21	22
23	24	25	26	27	28	29

Month 2

Sun	Mon	Tue	Wed	Thu	Fri	Sat
NM	1	2	3	4	5	6
7	8	9	10	11	12	13
14	15	16	17	18	19	20
21	22	23	24	25	26	27
28	29					

Month 3

Sun	Mon	Tue	Wed	Thu	Fri	Sat
		NM	1	2	3	4
5	6	7	8	9	10	11
12	13	14	15	16	17	18
19	20	21	22	23	24	25
26	27	28	29			

Month 4

Sun	Mon	Tue	Wed	Thu	Fri	Sat
				NM	1	2
3	4	5	6	7	8	9
10	11	12	13	14	15	16
17	18	19	20	21	22	23
24	25	26	27	28	29	

Month 5

Sun	Mon	Tue	Wed	Thu	Fri	Sat
						NM
1	2	3	4	5	6	7
8	9	10	11	12	13	14
15	16	17	18	19	20	21
22	23	24	25	26	27	28
29						

Month 6

Sun	Mon	Tue	Wed	Thu	Fri	Sat
	NM	1	2	3	4	5
6	7	8	9	10	11	12
13	14	15	16	17	18	19
20	21	22	23	24	25	26
27	28	29				

Month 7

Sun	Mon	Tue	Wed	Thu	Fri	Sat
			NM	1	2	3
4	5	6	7	8	9	10
11	12	13	14	15	16	17
18	19	20	21	22	23	24
25	26	27	28	29		

Month 8

Sun	Mon	Tue	Wed	Thu	Fri	Sat
					NM	1
2	3	4	5	6	7	8
9	10	11	12	13	14	15
16	17	18	19	20	21	22
23	2	25	26	27	28	29

Month 9

Sun	Mon	Tue	Wed	Thu	Fri	Sat
NM	1	2	3	4	5	6
7	8	9	10	11	12	13
14	15	16	17	18	19	20
21	22	23	24	25	26	27
28	29					

Month 10

Sun	Mon	Tue	Wed	Thu	Fri	Sat
		NM	1	2	3	4
5	6	7	8	9	10	11
12	13	14	15	16	17	18
19	20	21	22	23	24	25
26	27	28	29			

Month 11

Sun	Mon	Tue	Wed	Thu	Fri	Sat
				NM	1	2
3	4	5	6	7	8	9
10	11	12	13	14	15	16
17	18	19	20	21	22	23
24	25	26	27	28	29	

Month 12

Sun	Mon	Tue	Wed	Thu	Fri	Sat
						NM
1	2	3	4	5	6	7
8	9	10	11	12	13	14
15	16	17	18	19	20	21
22	23	24	25	26	27	28
29						

Year 5

Month 1

Sun	Mon	Tue	Wed	Thu	Fri	Sat
	NM	1	2	3	4	5
6	7	8	9	10	11	12
13	14	15	16	17	18	19
20	21	22	23	24	25	26
27	28	29				

Month 2

Sun	Mon	Tue	Wed	Thu	Fri	Sat
			NM	1	2	3
4	5	6	7	8	9	10
11	12	13	14	15	16	17
18	19	20	21	22	23	24
25	26	27	28	29		

Month 3

Sun	Mon	Tue	Wed	Thu	Fri	Sat
					NM	1
2	3	4	5	6	7	8
9	10	11	12	13	14	15
16	17	18	19	20	21	22
23	24	25	26	27	28	29

Month 4

Sun	Mon	Tue	Wed	Thu	Fri	Sat
NM	1	2	3	4	5	6
7	8	9	10	11	12	13
14	15	16	17	18	19	20
21	22	23	24	25	26	27
28	29					

Month 5

Sun	Mon	Tue	Wed	Thu	Fri	Sat
		NM	1	2	3	4
5	6	7	8	9	10	11
12	13	14	15	16	17	18
19	20	21	22	23	24	25
26	27	28	29			

Month 6

Sun	Mon	Tue	Wed	Thu	Fri	Sat
				NM	1	2
3	4	5	6	7	8	9
10	11	12	13	14	15	16
17	18	19	20	21	22	23
24	25	26	27	28	29	

Month 7

Sun	Mon	Tue	Wed	Thu	Fri	Sat
						NM
1	2	3	4	5	6	7
8	9	10	11	12	13	14
15	16	17	18	19	20	21
22	23	24	25	26	27	28
29						

Month 8

Sun	Mon	Tue	Wed	Thu	Fri	Sat
	NM	1	2	3	4	5
6	7	8	9	10	11	12
13	14	15	16	17	18	19
20	21	22	23	24	25	26
27	28	29				

Month 9

Sun	Mon	Tue	Wed	Thu	Fri	Sat
			NM	1	2	3
4	5	6	7	8	9	10
11	12	13	14	15	16	17
18	19	20	21	22	23	24
25	26	27	28	29		

Month 10

Sun	Mon	Tue	Wed	Thu	Fri	Sat
					NM	1
2	3	4	5	6	7	8
9	10	11	12	13	14	15
16	17	18	19	20	21	22
23	24	25	26	27	28	29

Month 11

Sun	Mon	Tue	Wed	Thu	Fri	Sat
NM	1	2	3	4	5	6
7	8	9	10	11	12	13
14	15	16	17	18	19	20
21	22	23	24	25	26	27
28	29					

Month 12

Sun	Mon	Tue	Wed	Thu	Fri	Sat
		NM	1	2	3	4
5	6	7	8	9	10	11
12	13	14	15	16	17	18
19	20	21	22	23	24	25
26	27	28	29			

By Mowreh IshiYAH YisraEL 2014

Year 6

Month 1

Sun	Mon	Tue	Wed	Thu	Fri	Sat
				NM	1	2
3	4	5	6	7	8	9
10	11	12	13	14	15	16
17	18	19	20	21	22	23
24	25	26	27	28	29	

Month 2

Sun	Mon	Tue	Wed	Thu	Fri	Sat
						NM
1	2	3	4	5	6	7
8	9	10	11	12	13	14
15	16	17	18	19	20	21
22/29	23	24	25	26	27	28

Month 3

Sun	Mon	Tue	Wed	Thu	Fri	Sat
	NM	1	2	3	4	5
6	7	8	9	10	11	12
13	14	15	16	17	18	19
20	21	22	23	24	25	26
27	28	29				

Month 4

Sun	Mon	Tue	Wed	Thu	Fri	Sat
			NM	1	2	3
4	5	6	7	8	9	10
11	12	13	14	15	16	17
18	19	20	21	22	23	24
25	26	27	28	29		

Month 5

Sun	Mon	Tue	Wed	Thu	Fri	Sat
					NM	1
2	3	4	5	6	7	8
9	10	11	12	13	14	15
16	17	18	19	20	21	22
23	24	25	26	27	28	29

Month 6

Sun	Mon	Tue	Wed	Thu	Fri	Sat
NM	1	2	3	4	5	6
7	8	9	10	11	12	13
14	15	16	17	18	19	20
21	22	23	24	25	26	27
28	29					

Month 7

Sun	Mon	Tue	Wed	Thu	Fri	Sat
		NM	1	2	3	4
5	6	7	8	9	10	11
12	13	14	15	16	17	18
19	20	21	22	23	24	25
26	27	28	29			

Month 8

Sun	Mon	Tue	Wed	Thu	Fri	Sat
				NM	1	2
3	4	5	6	7	8	9
10	11	12	13	14	15	16
17	18	19	20	21	22	23
24	25	26	27	28	29	

Month 9

Sun	Mon	Tue	Wed	Thu	Fri	Sat
						NM
1	2	3	4	5	6	7
8	9	10	11	12	13	14
15	16	17	18	19	20	21
22/29	23	24	25	26	27	28

Month 10

Sun	Mon	Tue	Wed	Thu	Fri	Sat
	NM	1	2	3	4	5
6	7	8	9	10	11	12
13	14	15	16	17	18	19
20	21	22	23	24	25	26
27	28	29				

Month 11

Sun	Mon	Tue	Wed	Thu	Fri	Sat
			NM	1	2	3
4	5	6	7	8	9	10
11	12	13	14	15	16	17
18	19	20	21	22	23	24
25	26	27	28	29		

Month 12

Sun	Mon	Tue	Wed	Thu	Fri	Sat
					NM	1
2	3	4	5	6	7	8
9	10	11	12	13	14	15
16	17	18	19	20	21	22
23	24	25	26	27	28	29

Year 7

Month 1

Sun	Mon	Tue	Wed	Thu	Fri	Sat
NM	1	2	3	4	5	6
7	8	9	10	11	12	13
14	15	16	17	18	19	20
21	22	23	24	25	26	27
28	29					

Month 2

Sun	Mon	Tue	Wed	Thu	Fri	Sat
		NM	1	2	3	4
5	6	7	8	9	10	11
12	13	14	15	16	17	18
19	20	21	22	23	24	25
26	27	28	29			

Month 3

Sun	Mon	Tue	Wed	Thu	Fri	Sat
				NM	1	2
3	4	5	6	7	8	9
10	11	12	13	14	15	16
17	18	19	20	21	22	23
24	25	26	27	28	29	

Month 4

Sun	Mon	Tue	Wed	Thu	Fri	Sat
						NM
1	2	3	4	5	6	7
8	9	10	11	12	13	14
15	16	17	18	19	20	21
22	23	24	25	26	27	28
29						

Month 5

Sun	Mon	Tue	Wed	Thu	Fri	Sat
	NM	1	2	3	4	5
6	7	8	9	10	11	12
13	14	15	16	17	18	19
20	21	22	23	24	25	26
27	28	29				

Month 6

Sun	Mon	Tue	Wed	Thu	Fri	Sat
			NM	1	2	3
4	5	6	7	8	9	10
11	12	13	14	15	16	17
18	19	20	21	22	23	24
25	26	27	28	29		

Month 7

Sun	Mon	Tue	Wed	Thu	Fri	Sat
					NM	1
2	3	4	5	6	7	8
9	10	11	12	13	14	15
16	17	18	19	20	21	22
23	24	25	26	27	28	29

Month 8

Sun	Mon	Tue	Wed	Thu	Fri	Sat
NM	1	2	3	4	5	6
7	8	9	10	11	12	13
14	15	16	17	18	19	20
21	22	23	24	25	26	27
28	29					

Month 9

Sun	Mon	Tue	Wed	Thu	Fri	Sat
		NM	1	2	3	4
5	6	7	8	9	10	11
12	13	14	15	16	17	18
19	20	21	22	23	24	25
26	27	28	29			

Month 10

Sun	Mon	Tue	Wed	Thu	Fri	Sat
				NM	1	2
3	4	5	6	7	8	9
10	11	12	13	14	15	16
17	18	19	20	21	22	23
24	25	26	27	28	29	

Month 11

Sun	Mon	Tue	Wed	Thu	Fri	Sat
						NM
1	2	3	4	5	6	7
8	9	10	11	12	13	14
15	16	17	18	19	20	21
22	23	24	25	26	27	28
29						

Month 12

Sun	Mon	Tue	Wed	Thu	Fri	Sat
	NM	1	2	3	4	5
6	7	8	9	10	11	12
13	14	15	16	17	18	19
20	21	22	23	24	25	26
27	28	29				

By Mowreh IshiYAH YisraEL 2014

Abib יהוה מוֹעֲדֵי 1st Year
YAHWEH'S SET TIMES

Yom Echad	Yom Sheniy	Yom Shliyshiy	Yom Rbiy'iy	Yom Chamiyshiy	Yom Shishshiy	Yom Shabbat
The Day YAH Created Light Gen. 1:1-5 Day One	The Day YAH Created the Heavens Gen. 1:6-8 Day Two	The Day YAH Created the Sea, Earth, Grass, Herbs, and Trees Gen. 1:9-13 Day Three	The Day YAH Created the Lights Gen. 1:14-19 Day of the 1st Month Day Four	1 The Day YAH Created sea creatures and Fowls of the Air Gen 1:20-23 Day Five	2 The Day YAH created creeping things, beast, and Man on Earth Gen 1:24-31 Day Six	3 The Day YAH ceased from his work and sanctified this day; the First Sabbath Day: Gen. 2:1-3 Day Seven
4 Day 4	5	6	7	8	9	10
11	12	13	14 Passover/Pesach	15 Chag Matzo/ Feast of Unleavened Bread Day 1	16 Day 2	17 Day 3
18	19 Day 5	20 Day 6	21 Day 7	22	23	24
25	26	27	28	29		

2nd Month

1st Year

יהוה מוֹעֲדֵי

YAHWEH'S SET TIMES

Yom Echad	Yom Sheniy	Yom Shliyshiy	Yom Rbiy'iy	Yom Chamiyshiy	Yom Shishshiy	Yom Shabbat
					Day of the 2nd Month	1
2	3	4	5	6	7	8
9	10	11	12	13	14	15
16 — 1st Day YAH Fed YisraEL with Manna Exodus 16	17	18	19	20	21	22 — YAHWEH Teaches YisraEL about the Shabbat Exodus 16
23	24	25	26	27	28	29

3rd Month — 1st Year

יהוה מוֹעֲדֵי — YAHWEH'S SET TIMES

Yom Echad	Yom Sheniy	Yom Shliyshiy	Yom Rbiy'iy	Yom Chamiyshiy	Yom Shishshiy	Yom Shabbat
Day of the 3rd Month	1	2 **The Day YAH Spoke to YisraEl out of Heaven and made a Covenant With YisraEl Exodus 19:1-10**	3	4	5	6 **Moshe went to receive the 10 Commandments Exodus 24**
7	8	9	10	11	12	13
14	15	16	17	18	19	20
21	22	23	24	25	26	27
28	29					

4th Month

יהוה מועדי
YAHWEH'S SET TIMES

1st Year

Yom Echad	Yom Sheniy	Yom Shliyshiy	Yom Rbiy'iy	Yom Chamiyshiy	Yom Shishshiy	Yom Shabbat
		Day of the 4th Month	1		2	3	4
5	6	7	8	9	10	11
12	13	14	15	16 **The Day Moshe Came Down From Receiving the First Set of 10 Commandments**	17	18
19	20	21	22	23	24	25
26	27	28	29			

5th Month — 1st Year

יהוה מועדי
YAHWEH'S SET TIMES

Yom Echad	Yom Sheniy	Yom Shliyshiy	Yom Rbiy'iy	Yom Chamiyshiy	Yom Shishshiy	Yom Shabbat
				Day of the 5th Month	1	2
3	4	5	6	7	8	9
10	11	12	13	14	15	16
17	18	19	20	21	22	23
24	25	26	27	28	29	

6th Month   1st
יהוה מועדי
YAHWEH'S SET TIMES   Year

Yom Echad	Yom Sheniy	Yom Shliyshiy	Yom Rbiy'iy	Yom Chamiyshiy	Yom Shishshiy	Yom Shabbat
1	2	3	4	5	6	7 Day of 6th Month
8	9	10	11	12	13	14
15	16	17	18	19	20	21
22	23	24	25	26	27	28
29						

7th Month 1st Year

יְהוָה מוֹעֲדֵי
YAHWEH'S SET TIMES

Yom Echad	Yom Sheniy	Yom Shliyshiy	Yom Rbiy'iy	Yom Chamiyshiy	Yom Shishshiy	Yom Shabbat
	Day of the 7th Month	**Yom Teruah** 1	2	3	4	5
6	7	8	9 **Fast of Yom Kippur Begins at Even**	10 **YOM KIPPUR**	11	12
13	14	15 **CHAG Succoth Day 1**	16 Day 2	17 Day 3	18 Day 4	19 Day 5
20 Day 6	21 Day 7	22 **Sabbath of Solemnity**	23	24	25	26
27	28	29				Yom Echad

8th Month 1st Year

יְהֹוָה מוֹעֲדֵי

YAHWEH'S SET TIMES

Yom Echad	Yom Sheniy	Yom Shliyshiy	Yom Rbiy'iy	Yom Chamiyshiy	Yom Shishshiy	Yom Shabbat
			Day of the 8th Month	1	2	3
4	5	6	7	8	9	10
11	12	13	14	15	16	17
18	19	20	21	22	23	24
25	26	27	28	29		

9th Month

יהוה מועדי
YAHWEH'S SET TIMES

1st Year

Yom Echad	Yom Sheniy	Yom Shliyshiy	Yom Rbiy'iy	Yom Chamiyshiy	Yom Shishshiy	Yom Shabbat
					Day of the 9th Month	1
2	3	4	5	6	7	8
9	10	11	12	13	14	15
16	17	18	19	20	21	22
23	24	25	26	27	28	29

10th Month

1st Year

יהוה מועדי
YAHWEH'S SET TIMES

Yom Echad	Yom Sheniy	Yom Shliyshiy	Yom Rbiy'iy	Yom Chamiyshiy	Yom Shishshiy	Yom Shabbat
Day of the 10th Month	1	2	3	4	5	6
7	8	9	10	11	12	13
14	15	16	17	18	19	20
21	22	23	24	25	26	27
28	29					

11th Month 1st Year

יהוה מועדי

YAHWEH'S SET TIMES

Yom Echad	Yom Sheniy	Yom Shliyshiy	Yom Rbiy'iy	Yom Chamiyshiy	Yom Shishshiy	Yom Shabbat
		Day of the 11th Month	1	2	3	4
5	6	7	8	9	10	11
12	13	14	15	16	17	18
19	20	21	22	23	24	25
26	27	28	29			

12th Month / 1st Year

יְהוָה מוֹעֲדֵי YAHWEH'S SET TIMES

Yom Echad	Yom Sheniy	Yom Shliyshiy	Yom Rbiy'iy	Yom Chamiyshiy	Yom Shishshiy	Yom Shabbat
				Day of the 12th Month	1	2
3	4	5	6	7	8	9
10	11	12	13	14	15	16
17	18	19	20	21	22	23
24	25	26	27	28	29	

Made in the USA
Middletown, DE
29 May 2022